THE MYSTERIES OF CHRIST

A SCRIPTURAL ROSARY

Compiled by Nancy Sabbag

the**WORD**®
among us

The Word Among Us
9639 Doctor Perry Road
Ijamsville, Maryland 21754
www.wordamongus.org
ISBN: 1-59325-027-4

Cover and book design: David Crosson
Art taken from *The Stein Quadryptich: Life & Death of Christ*, by Simon Bening,
The Walters Art Museum, Baltimore, Maryland

Made and printed in the United States of America

Library of Congress Control Number: 2003115009

Nihil obstat: Reverend Monsignor Vincent J. Haut, VG
Censor Librorum
October 30, 2003

Imprimatur: +Most Reverend Victor Galeone
Bishop of St. Augustine, Florida
October 30, 2003

Contents

THE *R* OSARY

A TREASURED DEVOTION

OF THE CHURCH

Catholics today are well acquainted with the practice of praying the holy rosary. Since the Middle Ages, faithful Christians have prayed various forms of the rosary to commemorate and savor the most important events of our Christian faith. "Simple yet profound, it still remains, at the dawn of this third millennium, a prayer of great significance, destined to bring forth a harvest of holiness," Pope John Paul II has said of this traditional and popular devotion (*Rosarium Virginis Mariae*, 1).

The rosary's beauty and appeal through the ages stem from its usefulness in helping believers meditate on the spiritual "mysteries" of the life, death, and glory of Christ. The rosary is a unique blend of vocal prayers with contemplative themes. Each "mystery" calls to mind one aspect of the Lord's work of redemption: his coming in the flesh; his earthly ministry; his death on the cross for our sins; and his resurrection and ascension into heaven. As we pray, focused on the events of a particular mystery, we enter into a divine journey with Jesus, our Emmanuel, accompanied by Mary, his blessed mother.

How to Pray the Rosary

The rosary is simple to pray. If you own a rosary, you know it is made up of a circular loop of fifty-four beads, connected at one juncture with a shorter strand of five beads, adorned by a crucifix at the end. The beads are placed in a repetitive pattern around the loop and are positioned in five "decades," or five groups of ten, with a single bead between each group. One *Hail Mary* is said for each of the ten beads in a decade, and one *Our Father* for each single bead in between. While praying, the person contemplates the mystery that the decade represents. Each rosary is begun with a sign of the cross and the *Apostles' Creed*, usually said while holding the crucifix. A *Gloria* is said after each set of *Hail Marys*. The rosary is often concluded with the prayer *Hail, Holy Queen*. Mentally dwelling on these mysteries while reverently repeating these prayers provides a rich devotional experience.

The Scriptural Rosary

The scriptural rosary has its roots in earlier forms of prayer popular throughout western Christendom. In the Middle Ages, before Christians prayed the rosary as we know it today, people used beads to pray "psalters," or a series of praises in honor of Jesus and Mary based on the interpretation of the 150 psalms in Scripture. For each of 150 beads (and later fifty beads), believers contemplated the deep meanings and prophecies of Christ within the psalms. This was the beginning of the mysteries. Later, the Dominicans popularized the convention of praying 150 *Hail Marys* and attaching a "little thought" or meditation from Jesus' or Mary's life to each. This is the model on which today's scriptural rosary is based.

When we pray a scriptural rosary, we assign a little thought to each *Hail Mary* and each *Our Father*. The difference is that each thought is a direct quote from Scripture. The Scripture verses are read before each prayer and are meant to unfold the story of Christ contained in that mystery. The passages of Scripture included in this book were taken from the gospel stories, epistles from the New Testament, prophetic sayings from the Old Testament, and the psalms. Together, these Scriptures paint a vivid picture of the mystery's meaning and its relevance to us today.

The New Mysteries

Traditionally, the rosary has commemorated fifteen mysteries: five Joyful Mysteries, five Sorrowful Mysteries, and five Glorious Mysteries of Christ. In October 2002, Pope John Paul II expanded the rosary with the addition of five new Luminous Mysteries or "Mysteries of Light." These mysteries commemorate the public life of Jesus, his ministry, and his mission as "the light of the world."

In his apostolic letter *Rosarium Virginis Mariae*, the Holy Father proclaimed a Year of the Rosary, from October 2002 to October 2003, and expressed his desire that during this time, "the rosary should be especially emphasized and promoted in the various Christian communities" (3). In the letter, the pope strongly encouraged the praying of the rosary, noting that it helps believers to contemplate the mystery of the Christian faith as well as to grow in holiness and in the art of prayer. Calling the rosary an "exquisitely contemplative prayer," the pope said that "without this contemplative dimension, it would lose its meaning." As Pope Paul VI once observed, "Without contemplation, the rosary is a body without a soul, and its recitation runs the risk of becoming a mechanical repetition of formulas" (12).

Our hope is that this scriptural rosary will be useful in adding a soulful dimension to your prayer. May it draw you nearer and nearer to Jesus, whose life and glory it honors, and to his mother Mary, who teaches us to contemplate the face of her Son.

THE MYSTERIES OF THE ROSARY

The Five Joyful Mysteries
1. The Annunciation
2. The Visitation
3. The Nativity
4. The Presentation
5. The Finding of Jesus in the Temple

The Five Luminous Mysteries
1. The Baptism of the Lord in the Jordan
2. The Wedding at Cana
3. The Proclamation of the Kingdom
4. The Transfiguration
5. The Institution of the Eucharist

The Five Sorrowful Mysteries
1. The Agony in the Garden
2. The Scourging
3. The Crowning with Thorns
4. The Carrying of the Cross
5. The Crucifixion

The Five Glorious Mysteries
1. The Resurrection
2. The Ascension
3. The Descent of the Holy Spirit
4. The Assumption of Mary
5. The Coronation of Mary

The Holy Father has suggested praying the Joyful Mysteries on Mondays and Saturdays; the Luminous Mysteries on Thursdays; the Sorrowful Mysteries on Tuesdays and Fridays, and the Glorious Mysteries on Wednesdays and Sundays.

THE PRAYERS

OF THE ROSARY

The Apostles' Creed

I believe in God, the Father almighty, creator of heaven and earth.

I believe in Jesus Christ, God's only Son, our Lord, who was conceived by the Holy Spirit, born of the Virgin Mary, suffered under Pontius Pilate, was crucified, died, and was buried; he descended to the dead. On the third day he rose again; he ascended into heaven. He is seated at the right hand of the Father, and he will come again to judge the living and the dead.

I believe in the Holy Spirit, the holy Catholic Church, the communion of saints, the forgiveness of sins, the resurrection of the body, and the life everlasting. Amen.

The Our Father

Our Father, who art in heaven, hallowed be thy name. Thy kingdom come, thy will be done on earth as it is in heaven. Give us this day our daily bread, and forgive us our trespasses as we forgive those who trespass against us. And lead us not into temptation but deliver us from evil. Amen.

The Hail Mary

Hail Mary, full of grace, the Lord is with you. Blessed are you among women, and blessed is the fruit of your womb, Jesus. Holy Mary, Mother of God, pray for us sinners, now and at the hour of our death. Amen.

The Gloria

Glory be to the Father, and to the Son, and to the Holy Spirit. As it was in the beginning, is now, and ever shall be, world without end. Amen.

The Hail, Holy Queen

Hail, holy Queen, Mother of Mercy, our life, our sweetness, and our hope. To you do we cry, poor banished children of Eve; to you do we send up our sighs, mourning, and weeping in this valley of tears. Turn, then, most gracious advocate, your eyes of mercy toward us, and after this, our exile, show unto us the blessed fruit of your womb, Jesus. O clement, O loving, O sweet Virgin Mary.

Pray for us, O Holy Mother of God, that we may be made worthy of the promises of Christ.

Fatima Prayer

O My Jesus, forgive us our sins, save us from the fires of hell, and lead all souls to heaven, especially those most in need of your mercy.

PRAYING TO THE RHYTHM OF THE ROSARY

By Joe Difato

What do you suppose would happen if someone were to mention the title of your favorite song? Wouldn't you, almost unconsciously, begin hearing the tune in your mind? Maybe you'd even start tapping your toes to the rhythm and humming along with the music. All it took was the mention of one song, and suddenly your body has begun to act differently.

Think also about the last time you saw a football game—whether live or on television. Immediately after a stunning play, doesn't the crowd go wild? Don't you see people jumping up and down or shouting out their approval? Who knows? Maybe you even join in the celebration yourself. You're so excited by what you've just seen, you can't help but make some noise. On a more spiritual note, Scripture is filled with stories of people who have been led to kneel or bow down when they have a powerful experience of God's presence in their midst.

All these examples can help us understand how praying the rosary can bring us to new depths of faith as we engage our bodies as well as our minds in praying through the great mysteries of the gospel. Let's take a look at how this can happen, beginning with the relationship between body and soul that these examples illustrate.

The Concept of Body and Soul. As we begin to look at body and soul, we should be careful not to overemphasize the differences between them. Both the Bible and the Church teach that body and soul are fully unified within the human person. For instance, when Genesis speaks of the first man and woman formed from earth and brought to life with the "breath of life" by God, it also teaches that human beings are made "in the image and likeness of God." Although we are complex beings, "fearfully and wondrously made," each of us still mirrors God's unity and oneness (Genesis 1:27; 2:7; Psalm 139:14).

We are all familiar with the makeup of our bodies: our physical shape, our internal organs, and the marvelous complexity of our circulatory or respiratory systems. We know that to stay healthy, we need the right balance of food, sleep, and exercise. We also know that just as a child's body grows and develops over time, so too will our bodies grow old and slow down with time.

It is through our bodies that we relate to the world around us: We see with our eyes, feel things with our hands, and taste with our tongues. Our bodies are also the means by which we communicate with one another. A simple touch of the hand can express a wealth of emotions—from grief and sadness to joy and gratitude. With the words coming out of our mouths, we tell others what we think and who we are, just as we use our ears to listen to those around us.

Just as the body reflects these "outer dimensions" of our lives, the soul reflects the more "inner dimensions." It's through the various faculties of the soul that we understand the things we experience in the world around us. It's through the soul, for instance, that we learn and remember, and it's through the soul that we imagine and dream, contemplate and choose. The soul receives data from the body, analyzes it, and decides how the body should react to what it has experienced. For instance, if we think about the example of the football game, we can tell that the body is doing the jumping and shouting, but it is because the soul has understood that a really exciting play had just been made. Without the soul's understanding, there would be no reaction of the body. And without the body's reaction, there would be no way we could show other people what we think about what we've just seen.

As amazing as all these functions are, one dimension outshines all of them. Because we are created in the image of God, we are spiritual beings as well as physical and psychological beings. We all have the potential to communicate, not just with those around us but even with God himself. It is through the spiritual dimensions of our nature that we can hear God's voice, experience his love, and undergo a transformation in our lives that can make us more and more like Jesus every day. This spiritual dimension has been called our "spirit," our "inner self," and even our "heart."

Soul and Body and the Rosary. How does all this relate to the rosary? In its most basic form, the rosary is a series of prayers to be recited in an established pattern. We know these prayers by heart, and the words come quickly to our memories. We usually don't have to think about them very much. However, if we were to pray the rosary on this level only, we might be keeping our bodies busy—our lips forming the words and our hands fingering the beads—but not really engaging our souls in the fullest way possible (1 Corinthians 14:14).

But it's precisely because it involves our bodies in this way that the rosary can be so effective a way to pray. Remember, we are physical as well as spiritual beings. We are not unattached souls who can successfully direct our thoughts without any help from our bodies. We've all had the experience of trying to relax in prayer, hoping that the distractions of life will fade away—only to find ourselves either nodding off to sleep or filled with yet another set of distractions.

We've also had the experience of coming upon important insights while we were driving somewhere, or shopping, or exercising, or even watching television. Haven't there been times when your body has been occupied and active, making it easier for your soul to focus on higher questions? It is sometimes when our bodies absorb some of the "fringe energy" of our hectic lives that our souls are freed up to focus on higher things (Colossians 3:1-2).

This is part of the reason why gestures like kneeling, standing, singing, and even dancing are such an ancient part of our tradition. In a very real way, our bodies need to become engaged in prayer just as our minds do—and this is precisely how the rosary works. Outwardly, we may be kneeling and reciting prayers. But inwardly, we have a great opportunity to ponder the mysteries of the gospel and to know intimacy with Jesus. So, when we are praying the rosary, we are allowing our bodies to become occupied with the rhythm of the prayers so that we can free our souls to draw closer to Jesus and treasure his love and his presence.

"When I Was a Child." Have you ever noticed how appealing the rosary can be to young children? The prayers are so simple, and even praying just one decade can give them a sense of accomplishment at having spent time with God. It's not uncommon for children to feel secure and peaceful, that God is on their side, as they pray through the rosary. Not surprisingly, much of this sense of satisfaction comes because the rosary offers them a simple structure for prayer and because it can feed their imaginations with stories about Jesus.

Much the same can be said for adults, but with another, deeper dimension added in. As the apostle Paul wrote, when we were children, we thought and acted like children. But as we grow up, we learn how to move beyond the ways of childhood and embrace the excitement and responsibilities of adulthood (1 Corinthians 13:11). In the realm of faith, it's as we grow up into Christ (Ephesians 4:15) that we can begin to experience the potential within the rosary to bring us to an ever-deepening understanding of Christ. The more we grow up, the more fully engaged our souls can become in prayer. Childlike joy can grow into a deep, abiding peace and confidence in God's love. Simplistic faith can develop into simple trust, enabling us to weather every storm of life. Knowing about Jesus can evolve into knowing him with an ever-increasing intimacy.

Mary knew Jesus more intimately than any other person. She watched him grow and develop. She witnessed his miracles, heard him preach, watched him die, and rejoiced in his resurrection. In a unique way, Mary shared in all the joys, sorrows, and glories of Jesus because her whole life was fixed on him. So, when we pray the rosary with hearts open to pondering the same mysteries Mary experienced, we too can fix our hearts on Jesus and come to know him as Mary did.

Penetrating the Mysteries. For centuries, people have experienced Jesus' love and transformation as they used the rosary to meditate on his birth, death, and resurrection. Now, Pope John Paul II has added the Mysteries of Light, which focus on five significant moments during Jesus' public ministry. He is convinced that praying the rosary—including these new mysteries—can help us become more like Jesus. He is convinced that as we contemplate the gospel in this way, we will be united more and more intimately to Jesus. Dwelling on the mysteries of the rosary is a powerful way for the Spirit to penetrate beyond the surface of our lives and lift us up to heaven.

GAZING UPON THE FACE OF CHRIST WITH MARY

Excerpts from Pope John Paul II's Apostolic Letter
Rosarium Virginis Mariae

The Rosary of the Virgin Mary, which gradually took form in the second millennium under the guidance of the Spirit of God, is a prayer loved by countless saints and encouraged by the Magisterium. . . . Though clearly Marian in character, the rosary is at heart a Christocentric prayer. In the sobriety of its elements, it has all the depth of the gospel message in its entirety. . . . It is an echo of the prayer of Mary, her perennial *Magnificat* for the work of the redemptive Incarnation which began in her virginal womb. With the rosary, the Christian people *sits at the school of Mary* and is led to contemplate the beauty on the face of Christ and to experience the depths of his love. Through the rosary the faithful receive abundant grace, as though from the very hands of the Mother of the Redeemer. (1)

A Face as Radiant as the Sun. *"And he was transfigured before them, and his face shone like the sun"* (Matthew 17:2). The gospel scene of Christ's transfiguration, in which the three apostles appear entranced by the beauty of the Redeemer, can be seen as *an icon of Christian contemplation.* To look upon the face of Christ, to recognize its mystery amid the daily events and the sufferings of his human life, and then to grasp the divine splendor definitively revealed in the risen

Lord: This is the task of every follower of Christ and therefore the task of each one of us. (9)

The contemplation of Christ has an *incomparable model* in Mary. In a unique way, the face of the Son belongs to Mary. It was in her womb that Christ was formed, receiving from her a human resemblance that points to an even greater spiritual closeness. No one has ever devoted himself to the contemplation of the face of Christ as faithfully as Mary. The eyes of her heart already turned to him at the Annunciation, when she conceived him by the power of the Holy Spirit. In the months that followed, she began to sense his presence and to picture his features. When at last she gave birth to him in Bethlehem, her eyes were able to gaze tenderly on the face of her Son, as she "wrapped him in swaddling cloths, and laid him in a manger" (Luke 2:7).

Thereafter, Mary's gaze, ever filled with adoration and wonder, would never leave him. At times it would be a *questioning look*, as in the episode of the finding in the Temple: "Son, why have you treated us so?" (Luke 2:48). It would always be a *penetrating gaze*, one capable of deeply understanding Jesus, even to the point of perceiving his hidden feelings and anticipating his decisions, as at Cana (John 2:5). At other times it would be a *look of sorrow*, especially beneath the cross (19:26-27). On the morning of Easter, hers was *a gaze radiant with the joy of the resurrection.* Finally, on the day of Pentecost, it was a *gaze afire* with the outpouring of the Spirit (Acts 1:14). (10)

Contemplating the scenes of the rosary in union with Mary is a means of learning from her to "read" Christ—to discover his secrets and to understand his message. This school of Mary is all the more effective if we consider that she teaches by obtaining for us in abundance the gifts of the Holy Spirit, even as she offers us the incomparable example of her own "pilgrimage of faith." As we contemplate each mystery of her Son's life, she invites us to do as she did at the

Annunciation: to ask humbly the questions which open us to the light, in order to end with the obedience of faith: "Behold, I am the handmaid of the Lord; be it done to me according to your word" (Luke 1:38). (14)

The Rosary, "A Compendium of the Gospel." The only way to approach the contemplation of Christ's face is by listening in the Spirit to the Father's voice, since "no one knows the Son except the Father" (Matthew 11:27). In the region of Caesarea Philippi, Jesus responded to Peter's confession of faith by indicating the source of that clear intuition of his identity: "Flesh and blood has not revealed this to you, but my Father who is in heaven" (16:17). What is needed, then, is a revelation from above. In order to receive that revelation, attentive listening is indispensable. . . .

The rosary is one of the traditional paths of Christian prayer directed to the contemplation of Christ's face. Pope Paul VI described it in these words: "As a gospel prayer, centered on the mystery of the redemptive incarnation, the rosary is a prayer with a clearly Christological orientation. Its most characteristic element, in fact, the litany-like succession of *Hail Marys*, becomes in itself an unceasing praise of Christ, who is the ultimate object both of the angel's announcement and of the greeting of the mother of John the Baptist: 'Blessed is the fruit of your womb' (Luke 1:42)." (18)

I believe that to bring out fully the Christological depths of the rosary it would be suitable to make an addition to the traditional pattern which, while left to the freedom of individuals and communities, could broaden it to include *the mysteries of Christ's public ministry between his baptism and his Passion*. . . . For the rosary to become more fully a "compendium of the gospel," it is fitting to add, following the Joyful Mysteries . . . a meditation on certain particularly significant moments in his public ministry—*the Mysteries of Light*. This addition of these new mysteries . . . is meant to give the rosary fresh life and to enkindle renewed interest in its place within Christian spirituality as a true doorway to the depths of the heart of Christ, ocean of joy and of light, of suffering and of glory. (19)

From "Mysteries" to the "Mystery": Mary's Way. The cycles of meditation proposed by the holy rosary are by no means exhaustive, but they do bring to mind what is essential, and they awaken in the soul a thirst for a knowledge of Christ continually nourished by the pure source of the gospel. Every individual event in the life of Christ, as narrated by the Evangelists, is resplendent with the Mystery that surpasses all understanding: the Mystery of the Word made flesh, in whom "all the fullness of God dwells bodily" (Ephesians 3:19; Colossians 2:9). For this reason, the *Catechism of the Catholic Church* places great emphasis on the mysteries of Christ, pointing out that "everything in the life of Jesus is a sign of his Mystery" (CCC, 515).

The rosary is at the service of this ideal; it offers the "secret" which leads easily to a profound and inward knowledge of Christ. We might call it *Mary's way*. It is the way of the example of the Virgin of Nazareth, a woman of faith, of silence, of attentive listening. It is also the way of a Marian devotion inspired by knowledge of the inseparable bond between Christ and his Blessed Mother: *the mysteries of Christ* are also in some sense *the mysteries of his Mother*, even when they do not involve her directly, for she lives from him and through him. By making our own the words of the angel Gabriel and St. Elizabeth contained in the *Hail Mary*, we find ourselves constantly drawn to seek out afresh in Mary, in her arms and in her heart, the "blessed fruit of her womb" (Luke 1:42). (24)

The Rosary, "A Treasure to Be Rediscovered." Dear brothers and sisters! A prayer so easy and yet so rich truly deserves to be rediscovered by the Christian community. . . . I look to all of you, brothers and sisters of every state of life, to you, Christian families, to you, the sick and elderly, and to you, young people: *confidently take up the rosary once again*. Rediscover the rosary in the light of Scripture, in harmony with the Liturgy, and in the context of your daily lives. (43)

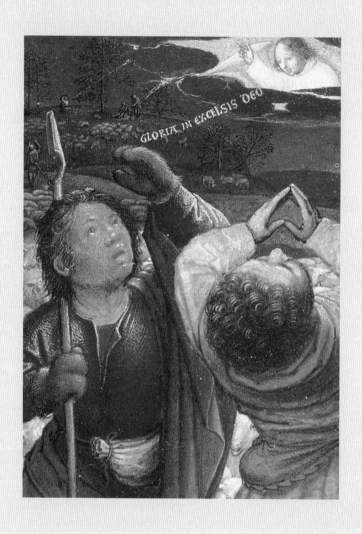

THE JOYFUL MYSTERIES

▶ The Sign of the Cross

▶ The Apostles' Creed

For to us a child is born, to us a son is given; . . . and his name will be called "Wonderful Counselor, Mighty God, Everlasting Father, Prince of Peace." ISAIAH 9:6

▶ Our Father

The zeal of the LORD of hosts will do this. ISAIAH 9:7

▶ Hail Mary for Faith

The God of heaven will set up a kingdom which shall never be destroyed . . . it shall stand for ever. DANIEL 2:44

▶ Hail Mary for Hope

No one has ever seen God; the only Son, who is in the bosom of the Father, he has made him known.
JOHN 1:18

▶ Hail Mary for Charity

▶ Glory Be to the Father...

First Joyful Mystery
THE ANNUNCIATION

*The angel Gabriel announces to
Mary the incarnation of Jesus by the power
of the Holy Spirit.*

In the sixth month, the angel Gabriel was sent from
God to a city of Galilee named Nazareth, to a virgin
betrothed to a man whose name was Joseph, of the
house of David; and the virgin's name was Mary.
LUKE 1:26-27

▶ Our Father...

And he came to her and said, "Hail, full of grace, the
Lord is with you!" LUKE 1:28

▶ Hail Mary...

"Behold, you will conceive in your womb and bear a
son, and you shall call his name Jesus." LUKE 1:31

▶ Hail Mary...

"He will be great, and will be called the Son of the Most High; and the Lord God will give to him the throne of his father David...and of his kingdom there will be no end." LUKE 1:32-33

▶ Hail Mary...

Mary said to the angel, "How can this be, since I have no husband?" And the angel said to her, "The Holy Spirit will come upon you, and the power of the Most High will overshadow you; therefore the child to be born will be called holy, the Son of God." LUKE 1:34-35

▶ Hail Mary...

Then Mary said, "Here am I, the servant of the Lord; let it be with me according to your word." Then the angel departed from her. LUKE 1:38

▶ Hail Mary...

Therefore the Lord himself will give you a sign. Behold, a young woman shall conceive and bear a son, and shall call his name Immanuel. ISAIAH 7:14

▶ Hail Mary...

The true light that enlightens every man was coming into the world. JOHN 1:9

▶ Hail Mary...

He is the image of the invisible God, the first-born of all creation. COLOSSIANS 1:15

▶ Hail Mary...

He had to be made like his brethren in every respect, so that he might become a merciful and faithful high priest in the service of God, to make expiation for the sins of the people. HEBREWS 2:17

▶ Hail Mary...

The LORD has done great things for us; we are glad. PSALM 126:3

▶ Hail Mary...

▶ Glory Be to the Father...

▶ O My Jesus...

Second Joyful Mystery
THE VISITATION

Mary visits her cousin Elizabeth.

In those days Mary arose and went with haste into the hill country, to a city of Judah, and she entered the house of Zechariah and greeted Elizabeth. LUKE 1:39-40

▶ Our Father...

And when Elizabeth heard the greeting of Mary, the babe leaped in her womb; and Elizabeth was filled with the Holy Spirit. LUKE 1:41

▶ Hail Mary...

And she exclaimed with a loud cry, "Blessed are you among women, and blessed is the fruit of your womb!" LUKE 1:42

▶ Hail Mary...

"And why is this granted me, that the mother of my Lord should come to me?" LUKE 1:43

▶ Hail Mary...

And Mary said, "My soul magnifies the Lord, and my spirit rejoices in God my Savior." LUKE 1:46-47

▶ Hail Mary…

"He who is mighty has done great things for me, and holy is his name." LUKE 1:49

▶ Hail Mary…

"And his mercy is on those who fear him from generation to generation." LUKE 1:50

▶ Hail Mary…

And now bless the God of all, who in every way does great things; who exalts our days from birth, and deals with us according to his mercy. SIRACH 50:22

▶ Hail Mary…

God chose what is foolish in the world to shame the wise; God chose what is weak in the world to shame the strong. 1 CORINTHIANS 1:27

▶ Hail Mary…

From his fullness we have all received, grace upon grace. JOHN 1:16

▶ Hail Mary…

I will sing to the LORD, because he has dealt bountifully with me. PSALM 13:6

▶ Hail Mary…

▶ Glory Be to the Father…

▶ O My Jesus…

Third Joyful Mystery
THE NATIVITY

Jesus is born in a manger in Bethlehem.

In those days a decree went out from Caesar Augustus
that all the world should be enrolled. And Joseph also
went . . . to the city of David, which is called Bethlehem
. . . to be enrolled with Mary, his betrothed, who was
with child. LUKE 2:1,4-5

▶ Our Father…

And while they were there, the time came for her to be
delivered. LUKE 2:6

▶ Hail Mary…

And she gave birth to her first-born son and wrapped him
in swaddling cloths, and laid him in a manger, because
there was no place for them in the inn. LUKE 2:7

▶ Hail Mary…

And in that region there were shepherds out in the field . . . And the angel said to them, "Be not afraid; for behold, I bring you good news of a great joy which will come to all the people; for to you is born this day in the city of David a Savior, who is Christ the Lord."
LUKE 2:8,10-11

▶ Hail Mary...

And suddenly there was with the angel a multitude of the heavenly host praising God and saying, "Glory to God in the highest, and on earth peace among men with whom he is pleased!" LUKE 2:13-14

▶ Hail Mary...

And they went with haste and found Mary and Joseph, and the babe lying in a manger. . . . And the shepherds returned, glorifying and praising God for all they had heard and seen, as it had been told them. LUKE 2:16,20

▶ Hail Mary...

But when the time had fully come, God sent forth his Son, born of woman, born under the law, to redeem those who were under the law, so that we might receive adoption as sons. GALATIANS 4:4-5

▶ Hail Mary...

But you, O Bethlehem Ephrathah, who are little to be among the clans of Judah, from you shall come forth for me one who is to be ruler in Israel, whose origin is from of old, from ancient days. MICAH 5:2

▶ Hail Mary…

There shall come forth a shoot from the stump of Jesse, and a branch shall grow out of his roots. And the Spirit of the LORD shall rest upon him. ISAIAH 11:1-2

▶ Hail Mary…

We have beheld his glory, glory as of the only Son from the Father. JOHN 1:14

▶ Hail Mary…

I have calmed and quieted my soul, like a child quieted at its mother's breast; like a child that is quieted is my soul. PSALM 131:2

▶ Hail Mary…

▶ Glory Be to the Father…

▶ O My Jesus…

Fourth Joyful Mystery

THE PRESENTATION

Mary and Joseph present Jesus in the Temple.

Now there was a man in Jerusalem, whose name was Simeon, and . . . it had been revealed to him by the Holy Spirit that he should not see death before he had seen the Lord's Christ. LUKE 2:25-26

▶ Our Father...

When the parents brought in the child Jesus . . . Simeon took him in his arms and praised God, saying, "Master, now you are dismissing your servant in peace, according to your word." LUKE 2:27-29

▶ Hail Mary...

"For my eyes have seen your salvation, which you have prepared in the presence of all peoples, a light for revelation to the Gentiles and for glory to your people Israel." LUKE 2:30-32

▶ Hail Mary...

Simeon blessed them and said to Mary his mother,
"Behold, this child is set for the fall and rising of many in
Israel . . . (and a sword will pierce through your own soul
also), that thoughts out of many hearts may be revealed."
LUKE 2:34-35

▶ Hail Mary...

And there was a prophetess, Anna . . . and coming up at
that very hour she gave thanks to God, and spoke of him
to all who were looking for the redemption of Jerusalem.
LUKE 2:36, 38

▶ Hail Mary...

"I am the LORD.... I have given you as a covenant to the
people, a light to the nations, to open the eyes that are
blind, to bring out the prisoners from the dungeon."
ISAIAH 42:6-7

▶ Hail Mary...

The LORD has bared his holy arm before the eyes of all
the nations; and all the ends of the earth shall see the salvation of our God. ISAIAH 52:10

▶ Hail Mary...

"Blessed are the eyes which see what you see! For I tell you that many prophets and kings desired to see what you see, and did not see it." LUKE 10:23-24

▶ Hail Mary…

The Lord whom you seek will suddenly come to his temple. MALACHI 3:1

▶ Hail Mary…

He has remembered his steadfast love and faithfulness to the house of Israel. All the ends of the earth have seen the victory of our God. PSALM 98:3

▶ Hail Mary…

Lift up your heads, O gates! and be lifted up, O ancient doors! that the King of glory may come in. Who is this King of glory? The LORD of hosts, he is the King of glory! PSALM 24:9-10

▶ Hail Mary…

▶ Glory Be to the Father…

▶ O My Jesus…

Fifth Joyful Mystery

THE FINDING OF JESUS IN THE TEMPLE

Mary and Joseph find Jesus teaching in the Temple.

Now his parents went to Jerusalem every year at the feast of the Passover. And when he was twelve years old, they went up according to custom. LUKE 2:41-42

▶ Our Father…

And when the feast was ended, as they were returning, the boy Jesus stayed behind in Jerusalem. His parents did not know it . . . and when they did not find him, they returned to Jerusalem, seeking him. LUKE 2:43, 45

▶ Hail Mary…

After three days they found him in the temple, sitting among the teachers, listening to them and asking them questions; and all who heard him were amazed at his understanding and his answers. LUKE 2:46-47

▶ Hail Mary…

When his parents saw him they were astonished; and his mother said to him, "Child, why have you treated us like this? Look, your father and I have been searching for you in great anxiety." LUKE 2:48

▶ Hail Mary…

He said to them, "Why were you searching for me? Did you not know that I must be in my Father's house?" LUKE 2:49

▶ Hail Mary…

And he went down with them and came to Nazareth, and was obedient to them; and his mother kept all these things in her heart. LUKE 2:51

▶ Hail Mary…

And Jesus increased in wisdom and in stature, and in favor with God and man. LUKE 2:52

▶ Hail Mary…

My soul yearns for thee in the night, my spirit within me earnestly seeks thee. ISAIAH 26:9

▶ Hail Mary…

You will seek me and find me; when you seek me with all your heart, I will be found by you, says the LORD. JEREMIAH 29:13-14

▶ Hail Mary…

I saw no temple in the city, for its temple is the Lord God the Almighty and the Lamb. REVELATION 21:22

▶ Hail Mary…

We ponder your steadfast love, O God, in the midst of your temple. PSALM 48:9

▶ Hail Mary…

▶ Glory Be to the Father…

▶ O My Jesus…

▶ Hail, Holy Queen…

THE **L**UMINOUS MYSTERIES

▶ The Sign of the Cross

▶ The Apostles' Creed

Arise, shine; for your light has come, and the glory of the LORD has risen upon you. ISAIAH 60:1

▶ Our Father

I will give you as a light to the nations, that my salvation may reach to the end of the earth. ISAIAH 49:6

▶ Hail Mary for Faith

The light shines in the darkness, and the darkness has not overcome it. JOHN 1:5

▶ Hail Mary for Hope

For once you were darkness, but now you are light in the Lord; walk as children of light. EPHESIANS 5:8

▶ Hail Mary for Charity

▶ Glory Be to the Father…

▶ O My Jesus…

First Luminous Mystery
THE BAPTISM OF THE LORD

John baptizes Jesus in the Jordan River.

In those days came John the Baptist, preaching in the wilderness of Judea, "Repent, for the kingdom of heaven is at hand." MATTHEW 3:1-2

▶ Our Father…

And there went out to him all the country of Judea, and all the people of Jerusalem; and they were baptized by him in the river Jordan, confessing their sins. MARK 1:5

▶ Hail Mary…

John bore witness to him, and cried, "This was he of whom I said, 'He who comes after me ranks before me, for he was before me.'" JOHN 1:15

▶ Hail Mary…

Then Jesus came from Galilee to the Jordan to John, to be baptized by him. MATTHEW 3:13

▶ Hail Mary…

John would have prevented him, saying, "I need to be baptized by you, and do you come to me?" But Jesus answered him, "Let it be so now; for thus it is fitting for us to fulfill all righteousness." MATTHEW 3:14-15

▶ Hail Mary...

And when Jesus had been baptized, just as he came up from the water, suddenly the heavens were opened to him and he saw the Spirit of God descending like a dove and alighting on him. MATTHEW 3:16

▶ Hail Mary...

And a voice came from heaven, "You are my Son, the Beloved; with you I am well pleased." MARK 1:11

▶ Hail Mary...

John [said], "I baptize you with water, but he who is mightier than I is coming, the thong of whose sandals I am not worthy to untie." LUKE 3:16

▶ Hail Mary...

The Spirit of the Lord GOD is upon me, because the LORD has anointed me to bring good tidings to the afflicted; he has sent me to bind up the brokenhearted, to proclaim liberty to the captives, and the opening of the prison to those who are bound. ISAIAH 61:1

▶ Hail Mary...

We were buried therefore with him by baptism into death, so that as Christ was raised from the dead by the glory of the Father, we too might walk in newness of life. ROMANS 6:4

▶ Hail Mary...

Let me hear what God the LORD will speak, for he will speak peace to his people, to his saints, to those who turn to him in their hearts. PSALM 85:8

▶ Hail Mary...

▶ Glory Be to the Father...

▶ O My Jesus...

Second Luminous Mystery
THE WEDDING AT CANA

At Mary's request, Jesus changes water into wine.

There was a marriage at Cana in Galilee, and the mother of Jesus was there; Jesus also was invited to the marriage, with his disciples. JOHN 2:1-2

▶ Our Father…

When the wine gave out, the mother of Jesus said to him, "They have no wine." JOHN 2:3

▶ Hail Mary…

And Jesus said to her, "Woman, what concern is that to you and to me? My hour has not yet come." JOHN 2:4

▶ Hail Mary…

His mother said to the servants, "Do whatever he tells you." JOHN 2:5

▶ Hail Mary…

Now six stone jars were standing there. . . . Jesus said to them, "Fill the jars with water." And they filled them up to the brim. He said to them, "Now draw some out, and take it to the steward of the feast." JOHN 2:6-8

▶ Hail Mary...

When the steward of the feast tasted the water now become wine . . . [he] called the bridegroom and said to him, "Every man serves the good wine first; and when men have drunk freely, then the poor wine; but you have kept the good wine until now." JOHN 2:9-10

▶ Hail Mary...

This, the first of his signs, Jesus did at Cana in Galilee, and manifested his glory; and his disciples believed in him. JOHN 2:11

▶ Hail Mary...

The people who walked in darkness have seen a great light; those who dwelt in a land of deep darkness, on them has light shined. ISAIAH 9:2

▶ Hail Mary...

Thus says the LORD: "In a time of favor I have answered you, in a day of salvation I have helped you. ISAIAH 49:8

▶ Hail Mary...

Now faith is the assurance of things hoped for, the conviction of things not seen. HEBREWS 11:1

▶ Hail Mary...

He sends forth his command to the earth; his word runs swiftly. PSALM 147:15

▶ Hail Mary...

▶ Glory Be to the Father...

▶ O My Jesus...

Third Luminous Mystery
THE PROCLAMATION OF THE KINGDOM

Jesus proclaims the coming of the Kingdom of God with the call to conversion and the forgiveness of sins.

Jesus came into Galilee, preaching the gospel of God, and saying "The time is fulfilled, and the kingdom of God is at hand; repent, and believe in the gospel." MARK 1:14-15

▶ Our Father…

And he went about all Galilee, teaching in their synagogues and preaching the gospel of the kingdom and healing every disease and every infirmity among the people. MATTHEW 4:23

▶ Hail Mary…

"Truly, I say to you, whoever does not receive the kingdom of God like a child shall not enter it." MARK 10:15

▶ Hail Mary…

"Not every one who says to me, 'Lord, Lord,' shall enter the kingdom of heaven, but he who does the will of my Father who is in heaven." MATTHEW 7:21

▶ Hail Mary…

They brought to him a paralytic, lying on his bed; and when Jesus saw their faith he said to the paralytic, "Take heart, my son; your sins are forgiven." MATTHEW 9:2

▶ Hail Mary…

Now some of the scribes were sitting there, questioning in their hearts, "Why does this man speak thus? It is blasphemy! Who can forgive sins but God alone?" MARK 2:6-7

▶ Hail Mary…

And immediately Jesus . . . said to them, "Which is easier, to say to the paralytic, 'Your sins are forgiven,' or to say, 'Rise, take up your pallet and walk'?" MARK 2:8-9

▶ Hail Mary…

And [the paralytic] rose and went home. MATTHEW 9:7

▶ Hail Mary…

"Blessed are the poor in spirit, for theirs is the kingdom of heaven." MATTHEW 5:3

▶ Hail Mary...

"Let your light so shine before men, that they may see your good works and give glory to your Father who is in heaven." MATTHEW 5:16

▶ Hail Mary...

This God—his way is perfect; the promise of the LORD is true. PSALM 18:30

▶ Hail Mary...

▶ Glory Be to the Father...

▶ O My Jesus...

Fourth Luminous Mystery
THE TRANSFIGURATION

Jesus is transfigured on Mount Tabor.

Jesus took with him Peter and James and John, and led them up a high mountain apart by themselves; and he was transfigured before them. MARK 9:2

▶ Our Father…

And his face shown like the sun, and his garments became white as light. MATTHEW 17:2

▶ Hail Mary…

Suddenly they saw two men, Moses and Elijah, talking to him. They appeared in glory and were speaking of his departure, which he was about to accomplish at Jerusalem. LUKE 9:30-31

▶ Hail Mary…

And Peter said to Jesus, "Lord, it is well that we are here; if you wish, I will make three booths here, one for you and one for Moses and one for Elijah."
MATTHEW 17:4

▶ Hail Mary...

As he said this, a cloud came and overshadowed them; and they were afraid as they entered the cloud.
LUKE 9:34

▶ Hail Mary...

And a voice from the cloud said, "This is my beloved Son, with whom I am well pleased; listen to him."
MATTHEW 17:5

▶ Hail Mary...

When the disciples heard this, they fell on their faces, and were filled with awe. But Jesus came and touched them, saying, "Rise, and have no fear." MATTHEW 17:6-7

▶ Hail Mary...

We did not follow cleverly devised myths when we made known to you the power and coming of our Lord Jesus Christ, but we were eyewitnesses of his majesty. 2 PETER 1:16

▶ Hail Mary...

Rejoice in so far as you share Christ's sufferings, that you may also rejoice and be glad when his glory is revealed. 1 PETER 4:13

▶ Hail Mary...

Ascribe to the LORD the glory of his name; worship the LORD in holy array. PSALM 29:2

▶ Hail Mary...

I have looked upon thee in the sanctuary, beholding thy power and glory. PSALM 63:2

▶ Hail Mary...

▶ Glory Be to the Father...

▶ O My Jesus...

Fifth Luminous Mystery
THE INSTITUTION OF THE EUCHARIST

Jesus changes bread and wine into his body and blood.

Now the feast of Unleavened Bread drew near, which is called the Passover. LUKE 22:1

▶ Our Father...

So Jesus sent Peter and John, saying, "Go and prepare the passover for us, that we may eat it." LUKE 22:8

▶ Hail Mary...

And the disciples did as Jesus had directed them, and they prepared the passover. When it was evening, he sat at table with his twelve disciples. MATTHEW 26:19-20

▶ Hail Mary...

And he said to them, "I have earnestly desired to eat this passover with you before I suffer; for I tell you I shall not eat it until it is fulfilled in the kingdom of God." LUKE 22:15-16

▶ Hail Mary...

And as they were eating, he took bread, and blessed, and broke it, and gave it to them, and said, "Take; this is my body." MARK 14:22

▶ Hail Mary...

And he took a cup, and when he had given thanks he gave it to them, and they all drank of it. And he said to them, "This is my blood of the covenant, which is poured out for many." MARK 14:23-24

▶ Hail Mary...

Jesus said to them, "Truly, truly, I say to you, unless you eat the flesh of the Son of man and drink his blood, you have no life in you; he who eats my flesh and drinks my blood has eternal life, and I will raise him up at the last day." JOHN 6:53-54

▶ Hail Mary...

Blessed are those who are invited to the marriage supper of the Lamb. REVELATION 19:9

▶ Hail Mary...

For as often as you eat this bread and drink the cup, you proclaim the Lord's death until he comes.

1 CORINTHIANS 11:26

▶ Hail Mary...

Yet he commanded the skies above, and opened the doors of heaven . . . Man ate of the bread of the angels; he sent them food in abundance.

PSALM 78:23,25

▶ Hail Mary...

How precious is your steadfast love, O God! All people may take refuge in the shadow of your wings. They feast on the abundance of your house, and you give them drink from the river of your delights.

PSALM 36:7-8

▶ Hail Mary...

▶ Glory Be to the Father...

▶ O My Jesus...

▶ Hail, Holy Queen...

THE  SORROWFUL MYSTERIES

▶ The Sign of the Cross

▶ The Apostles' Creed

Rejoice greatly, O daughter of Zion! Shout aloud, O daughter of Jerusalem! Lo, your king comes to you; triumphant and victorious is he, humble and riding on an ass, on a colt the foal of an ass. ZECHARIAH 9:9

▶ Our Father...

Though he had done so many signs before them, yet they did not believe in him. JOHN 12:37

▶ Hail Mary for Faith

And I, when I am lifted up from the earth, will draw all people to myself. JOHN 12:32

▶ Hail Mary for Hope

For I tell you that this scripture must be fulfilled in me, 'And he was reckoned with transgressors'; for what is written about me has its fulfillment. LUKE 22:37

▶ Hail Mary for Charity

▶ Glory Be to the Father...

▶ O My Jesus...

First Sorrowful Mystery
THE AGONY IN THE GARDEN

*Jesus prays in Gethsemane the night
before his crucifixion.*

Then Jesus went with them to a place called
Gethsemane; and he said to his disciples, "Sit here
while I go over there and pray." MATTHEW 26:36

▶ Our Father...

Then he withdrew from them about a stone's throw,
knelt down, and prayed, "Father, if you are willing,
remove this cup from me; yet, not my will but yours
be done." LUKE 22:41-42

▶ Hail Mary...

He said to Peter, "Simon, are you asleep? Could you
not watch one hour?" MARK 14:37

▶ Hail Mary...

"Watch and pray that you may not enter into temptation; the spirit indeed is willing, but the flesh is weak."
MARK 14:38

▶ Hail Mary…

In his anguish he prayed more earnestly, and his sweat became like great drops of blood falling down on the ground. LUKE 22:44

▶ Hail Mary…

Then he came to the disciples and said to them, "Are you still sleeping and taking your rest? See, the hour is at hand, and the Son of Man is betrayed into the hands of sinners." MATTHEW 26:45

▶ Hail Mary…

There came a crowd, and the man called Judas, one of the twelve, was leading them. He drew near to Jesus to kiss him; but Jesus said to him, "Judas, would you betray the Son of man with a kiss?" LUKE 22:47-48

▶ Hail Mary…

Then they seized him and led him away, bringing him into the high priest's house. LUKE 22:54

▶ Hail Mary…

Jesus said to them, "My food is to do the will of him who sent me, and to accomplish his work." JOHN 4:34

▶ Hail Mary...

In the days of his flesh, Jesus offered up prayers and supplications, with loud cries and tears, to him who was able to save him from death, and he was heard for his godly fear. HEBREWS 5:7

▶ Hail Mary...

You who fear the LORD, praise him! . . . For he has not despised or abhorred the affliction of the afflicted; and he has not hid his face from him, but has heard, when he cried to him. PSALM 22:23-24

▶ Hail Mary...

▶ Glory Be to the Father...

▶ O My Jesus...

Second Sorrowful Mystery
THE SCOURGING

Pilate has Jesus scourged.

Pilate said to him, "So you are a king?" JOHN 18:37

▶ Our Father...

Jesus answered, "You say that I am a king. For this I was born, and for this I have come into the world, to bear witness to the truth. Every one who is of the truth hears my voice." JOHN 18:37

▶ Hail Mary...

Then Pilate said to him, "Do you not hear how many things they testify against you?" But he gave him no answer, not even to a single charge; so that the governor wondered greatly. MATTHEW 27:13-14

▶ Hail Mary...

Pilate then called together the chief priests and the rulers of the people, and said to them, . . ."Behold, nothing deserving death has been done by him; I will therefore chastise him and release him." LUKE 23:13-16

▶ Hail Mary...

But they all cried out together, "Away with this man, and release to us Barabbas." LUKE 23:18

▶ Hail Mary...

Then Pilate took Jesus and scourged him. JOHN 19:1

▶ Hail Mary...

I gave my back to the smiters, and my cheeks to those who pulled out the beard; I hid not my face from shame and spitting. ISAIAH 50:6

▶ Hail Mary...

He was wounded for our transgressions; he was bruised for our iniquities; upon him was the chastisement that made us whole, and with his stripes we are healed. ISAIAH 53:5

▶ Hail Mary...

He was oppressed, and he was afflicted, yet he opened not his mouth; like a lamb that is led to slaughter, and like a sheep that before its shearers is dumb, so he opened not his mouth. ISAIAH 53:7

▶ Hail Mary…

Consider him who endured from sinners such hostility against himself, so that you may not grow weary or faint-hearted. HEBREWS 12:3

▶ Hail Mary…

Be strong, and let your heart take courage, all you who wait for the LORD. PSALM 31:24

▶ Hail Mary…

▶ Glory Be to the Father…

▶ O My Jesus…

Third Sorrowful Mystery
THE CROWNING
WITH THORNS

The soldiers mockingly place a crown of thorns on Jesus' head.

And they stripped him and put a scarlet robe upon him, and plaiting a crown of thorns they put it on his head, and put a reed in his right hand. MATTHEW 27:28-29

▶ Our Father…

And kneeling before him they mocked him, saying, "Hail, King of the Jews!" And they spat upon him, and took the reed and struck him on the head.
MATTHEW 27:29-30

▶ Hail Mary…

Pilate went out again, and said to them, "See, I am bringing him out to you, that you may know that I find no crime in him." JOHN 19:4

▶ Hail Mary…

So Jesus came out, wearing the crown of thorns and the purple robe. Pilate said to them, "Behold the man!"
JOHN 19:5

▶ Hail Mary…

When the chief priests and the officers saw him, they cried out, "Crucify him, crucify him!" JOHN 19:6

▶ Hail Mary…

Pilate said to them, "Shall I crucify your King?" The chief priests answered, "We have no king but Caesar." JOHN 19:15

▶ Hail Mary…

I am . . . scorned by men, and despised by the people. All who see me mock at me; they make mouths at me, they wag their heads. PSALM 22:6-7

▶ Hail Mary…

With a rod they strike upon the cheek the ruler of Israel. MICAH 5:1

▶ Hail Mary…

He was despised and rejected by others; a man of suffering and acquainted with infirmity; and as one from whom others hide their faces he was despised, and we held him of no account. ISAIAH 53:3

▶ Hail Mary…

But we see Jesus, who for a little while was made lower than the angels, crowned with glory and honor because of the suffering of death, so that by the grace of God he might taste death for every one. HEBREWS 2:9

▶ Hail Mary…

Be gracious to me, O LORD. See what I suffer from those who hate me; you are the one who lifts me up from the gates of death. PSALM 9:13

▶ Hail Mary…

▶ Glory Be to the Father…

▶ O My Jesus…

Fourth Sorrowful Mystery
THE CARRYING OF THE CROSS

A scourged and battered Jesus carries his cross to Calvary.

So they took Jesus, and he went out, bearing his own cross, to the place called the place of the skull, which is called in Hebrew Golgotha. JOHN 19:17

▶ Our Father…

As they went out, they came upon a man of Cyrene, Simon by name; this man they compelled to carry his cross. MATTHEW 27:32

▶ Hail Mary…

And there followed him a great multitude of the people, and of women who bewailed and lamented him.
LUKE 23:27

▶ Hail Mary…

But Jesus turning to them said, "Daughters of
Jerusalem, do not weep for me, but weep for yourselves
and for your children…. For if they do this when the
wood is green, what will happen when it is dry?"
LUKE 23:28,31

▶ Hail Mary…

And when they came to a place called Golgotha (which
means the place of a skull), they offered him wine to
drink, mingled with gall; but when he tasted it, he
would not drink it. MATTHEW 27:33-34

▶ Hail Mary…

Surely he has borne our griefs and carried our sorrows.
ISAIAH 53:4

▶ Hail Mary…

"If any man would come after me, let him deny himself
and take up his cross and follow me." MATTHEW 16:24

▶ Hail Mary…

"Take my yoke upon you, and learn from me; for I am
gentle and lowly in heart, and you will find rest for your
souls." MATTHEW 11:29

▶ Hail Mary…

Even though I walk through the darkest valley, I fear no evil; for you are with me; your rod and your staff—they comfort me. PSALM 23:4

 Hail Mary…

All we like sheep have gone astray; we have all turned to our own way, and the LORD has laid on him the iniquity of us all. ISAIAH 53:6

 Hail Mary…

The LORD has heard the sound of my weeping. The LORD has heard my supplication; the LORD accepts my prayer. PSALM 6:8-9

 Hail Mary…

 Glory Be to the Father…

 O My Jesus…

Fifth Sorrowful Mystery
THE CRUCIFIXION

Jesus is crucified and dies.

And when they came to the place which is called The
Skull, there they crucified him, and the criminals,
one on the right and one on the left. LUKE 23:33

▶ Our Father...

Pilate also wrote a title and put it on the cross; it read,
"Jesus of Nazareth, the King of the Jews." JOHN 19:19

▶ Hail Mary...

And those who passed by derided him, wagging their
heads and saying, "You who would destroy the temple
and build it in three days, save yourself! If you are the Son
of God, come down from the cross." MATTHEW 27:39-40

▶ Hail Mary...

When it was noon, darkness came over the whole land
until three in the afternoon. At three o'clock Jesus cried
out with a loud voice, "Eloi, Eloi, lema sabachthani?"
which means, "My God, my God, why have you forsaken
me?" MARK 15:33-34

▶ Hail Mary...

And the curtain of the temple was torn in two. Then Jesus, crying with a loud voice, said, "Father, into your hands I commend my spirit!" LUKE 23:45-46

▶ Hail Mary…

Having said this, he breathed his last. LUKE 23:46

▶ Hail Mary…

[He] emptied himself, taking the form of a slave, being born in human likeness. And being found in human form, he humbled himself and became obedient to the point of death— even death on a cross. PHILIPPIANS 2:7-8

▶ Hail Mary…

But God shows his love for us in that while we were yet sinners Christ died for us. ROMANS 5:8

▶ Hail Mary…

He himself bore our sins in his body on the tree, that we might die to sin and live to righteousness. By his wounds you have been healed. 1 PETER 2:24

▶ Hail Mary…

I have been crucified with Christ; it is no longer I who live, but Christ who lives in me; and the life I now live in the flesh I live by faith in the Son of God, who loved me and gave himself for me. GALATIANS 2:20

▶ Hail Mary…

My times are in your hand; deliver me from the hand of my enemies and persecutors. Let your face shine upon your servant; save me in your steadfast love.
PSALM 31:15-16

▶ Hail Mary…

▶ Glory Be to the Father…

▶ O My Jesus…

▶ Hail, Holy Queen…

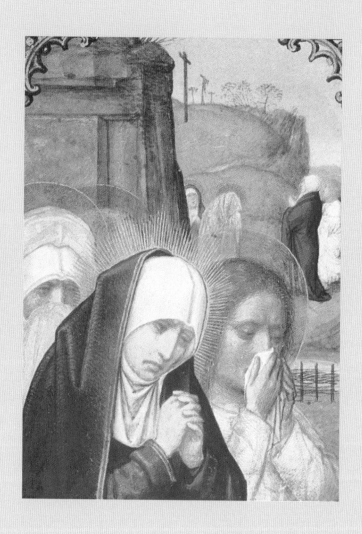

THE GLORIOUS MYSTERIES

▶ The Sign of the Cross

▶ The Apostles' Creed

O sing to the LORD a new song, for he has done marvelous things! His right hand and his holy arm have gotten him victory. PSALM 98:1

▶ Our Father

"Look at my hands and my feet; that it is I myself. Touch me and see; for a ghost does not have flesh and bones as you see that I have." LUKE 24:39

▶ Hail Mary for Faith

To the only God, our Savior through Jesus Christ our Lord, be glory, majesty, dominion, and authority, before all time and now and for ever. Amen. JUDE 25

▶ Hail Mary for Hope

Thanks be to God, who gives us the victory through our Lord Jesus Christ. 1 CORINTHIANS 15:57

▶ Hail Mary for Charity

▶ Glory Be to the Father...

▶ O My Jesus...

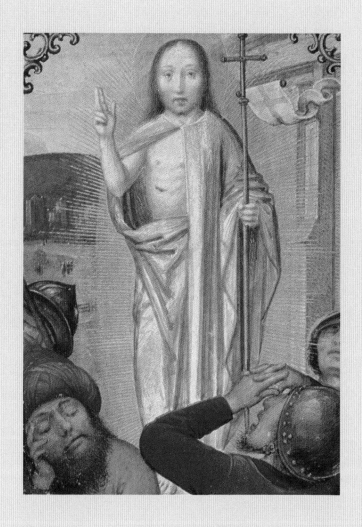

First Glorious Mystery
THE RESURRECTION

Jesus is raised from the dead three days after his death.

And when the sabbath was past, Mary Magdalene, and Mary the mother of James, and Salome, bought spices, so that they might go and anoint him. And very early on the first day of the week they went to the tomb when the sun had risen. MARK 16:1-2

▶ Our Father…

The angel said to the women, "Do not be afraid; for I know that you seek Jesus who was crucified. He is not here; for he has risen, as he said. Come, see the place where he lay." MATTHEW 28:5-6

▶ Hail Mary…

Simon Peter . . . went into the tomb. He saw the linen wrappings lying there, and the cloth that had been on Jesus' head, not lying with the linen wrappings but rolled up in a place by itself. JOHN 20:6-7

▶ Hail Mary…

Then the other disciple, who reached the tomb first, also went in, and he saw and believed. JOHN 20:8

▶ Hail Mary...

But Mary stood weeping outside the tomb. . . . She turned round and saw Jesus standing, but she did not know that it was Jesus. Jesus said to her, "Woman, why are you weeping? Whom do you seek?" JOHN 20:11,14-15

▶ Hail Mary...

Jesus said to her, "Do not hold me, for I have not yet ascended to the Father; but go to my brethren and say to them, I am ascending to my Father and your Father, to my God and your God." JOHN 20:17

▶ Hail Mary...

"I am the resurrection and the life; he who believes in me, though he die, yet shall he live, and whoever lives and believes in me shall never die." JOHN 11:25-26

▶ Hail Mary...

Blessed be the God and Father of our Lord Jesus Christ! By his great mercy we have been born anew to a living hope through the resurrection of Jesus Christ from the dead. 1 PETER 1:3

▶ Hail Mary...

If we have died with Christ, we believe that we shall also live with him. For we know that Christ being raised from the dead will never die again; death no longer has dominion over him. ROMANS 6:8-9

▶ Hail Mary…

Our God is a God of salvation; and to GOD, the Lord, belongs escape from death. PSALM 68:20

▶ Hail Mary…

You show me the path of life. In your presence there is fullness of joy; in your right hand are pleasures forevermore. PSALM 16:11

▶ Hail Mary…

▶ Glory Be to the Father…

▶ O My Jesus…

Second Glorious Mystery
THE ASCENSION

*Christ ascends into heaven forty days
after rising from the dead.*

So then the Lord Jesus, after he had spoken to them,
was taken up into heaven, and sat down at the right
hand of God. MARK 16:19

▶ Our Father...

Now the eleven disciples went to Galilee, to the mountain to which Jesus had directed them. . . . And Jesus
came and said to them, "All authority in heaven and
on earth has been given to me." MATTHEW 28:16,18

▶ Hail Mary...

"Go therefore and make disciples of all nations, bap-
tizing them in the name of the Father and of the Son
and of the Holy Spirit, teaching them to observe all
that I have commanded you." MATTHEW 28:19-20

▶ Hail Mary...

And remember, I am with you always, to the end of the age." MATTHEW 28:20

▶ Hail Mary…

"But you shall receive power when the Holy Spirit has come upon you; and you shall be my witnesses in Jerusalem and in all Judea and Samaria and to the end of the earth." ACTS 1:8

▶ Hail Mary…

And when he had said this, as they were looking on, he was lifted up, and a cloud took him out of their sight. ACTS 1:9

▶ Hail Mary…

And while they were gazing into heaven as he went, behold, two men stood by them in white robes, and said, "Men of Galilee, why do you stand looking into heaven? This Jesus, who was taken up from you into heaven, will come in the same way as you saw him go into heaven." ACTS 1:10-11

▶ Hail Mary…

Sing to God, O kingdoms of the earth . . . to him who rides in the heavens, the ancient heavens; lo, he sends forth his voice, his mighty voice. PSALM 68:32-33

▶ Hail Mary…

Since then we have a great high priest who has passed through the heavens, Jesus, the Son of God, let us hold fast our confession. HEBREWS 4:14

▶ Hail Mary...

The first man was from the earth, a man of dust; the second man is from heaven. . . . Just as we have borne the image of the man of dust, we will also bear the image of the man of heaven. 1 CORINTHIANS 15:47,49

▶ Hail Mary...

The LORD has established his throne in the heavens, and his kingdom rules over all. PSALM 103:19

▶ Hail Mary...

▶ Glory Be to the Father...

▶ O My Jesus...

Third Glorious Mystery
THE DESCENT OF THE HOLY SPIRIT

The Holy Spirit descends on the disciples at Pentecost.

When the day of Pentecost had come, they were all together in one place. And suddenly a sound came from heaven like the rush of a mighty wind, and it filled all the house where they were sitting. ACTS 2:1-2

▶ Our Father...

And there appeared to them tongues as of fire, distributed and resting on each one of them. ACTS 2:3

▶ Hail Mary...

And they were all filled with the Holy Spirit and began to speak in other tongues, as the Spirit gave them utterance. ACTS 2:4

▶ Hail Mary...

And at this sound the multitude came together, and they were bewildered, because each one heard them speaking in his own language. And they were amazed. ACTS 2:6-7

▶ Hail Mary...

And Peter said to them, "Repent, and be baptized every one of you in the name of Jesus Christ for the forgiveness of your sins; and you shall receive the gift of the Holy Spirit." ACTS 2:38

▶ Hail Mary…

"For the promise is to you and to your children and to all that are far off, every one whom the Lord our God calls to him." ACTS 2:39

▶ Hail Mary…

"I have baptized you with water; but he will baptize you with the Holy Spirit." MARK 1:8

▶ Hail Mary…

"And it shall come to pass afterward, that I will pour out my spirit on all flesh; your sons and your daughters shall prophesy, your old men shall dream dreams, and your young men shall see visions." JOEL 2:28

▶ Hail Mary…

God's love has been poured into our hearts through the Holy Spirit which has been given to us.
ROMANS 5:5

▶ Hail Mary…

And because you are children, God has sent the Spirit of his Son into our hearts, crying, "Abba! Father!" GALATIANS 4:6

▶ Hail Mary…

Cast me not away from thy presence, and take not thy holy Spirit from me. PSALM 51:11

▶ Hail Mary…

▶ Glory Be to the Father…

▶ O My Jesus…

Fourth Glorious Mystery
THE ASSUMPTION
OF MARY

At the end of her life, Mary is taken to heaven.

"Blessed is she who believed that there would be a fulfillment of what was spoken to her from the Lord."
LUKE 1:45

▶ Our Father…

And the angel said to her, "Do not be afraid, Mary, for you have found favor with God." LUKE 1:30

▶ Hail Mary…

A woman in the crowd raised her voice and said to [Jesus], "Blessed is the womb that bore you, and the breasts that you sucked!" LUKE 11:27

▶ Hail Mary…

My beloved speaks and says to me: "Arise, my love, my fair one, and come away; for now the winter is past, the rain is over and gone." SONG OF SONGS 2:10-11

▶ Hail Mary…

He sets on high those who are lowly, and those who mourn are lifted to safety. JOB 5:11

▶ Hail Mary…

He will rejoice over you with gladness, he will renew you in his love; he will exult over you with loud singing as on a day of festival. ZEPHANIAH 3:17-18

▶ Hail Mary…

And the dead in Christ will rise first; then we who are alive, who are left, shall be caught up together with them in the clouds to meet the Lord in the air; and so we shall always be with the Lord.
1 THESSALONIANS 4:16-17

▶ Hail Mary…

If for this life only we have hoped in Christ, we are of all men most to be pitied. But in fact Christ has been raised from the dead, the first fruits of those who have fallen asleep. 1 CORINTHIANS 15:19-20

▶ Hail Mary…

"O death, where is thy victory? O death, where is thy sting?" 1 CORINTHIANS 15:55

▶ Hail Mary…

[Be] imitators of those who through faith and patience inherit the promises. HEBREWS 6:12

▶ Hail Mary...

Praise the LORD from the heavens, praise him in the heights! Praise him, all his angels, praise him, all his host! Praise him, sun and moon, praise him, all you shining stars! PSALM 148:1-3

▶ Hail Mary...

▶ Glory Be to the Father...

▶ O My Jesus...

Fifth Glorious Mystery
THE CORONATION OF MARY

Mary is crowned as queen of heaven and earth.

And a great portent appeared in heaven, a woman clothed with the sun, with the moon under her feet, and on her head a crown of twelve stars.
REVELATION 12:1

▶ Our Father…

She brought forth a male child, one who is to rule all the nations with a rod of iron. REVELATION 12:5

▶ Hail Mary…

"Who is this that looks forth like the dawn, fair as the moon, bright as the sun?" SONG OF SONGS 6:10

▶ Hail Mary…

The princess is decked in her chamber with gold-woven robes; in many-colored robes she is led to the king. PSALM 45:13-14

▶ Hail Mary…

But the righteous live for ever, and their reward is with the Lord; the Most High takes care of them. WISDOM 5:15

▶ Hail Mary…

Therefore they will receive a glorious crown and a beautiful diadem from the hand of the Lord, because with his right hand he will cover them, and with his arm he will shield them. WISDOM 5:16

▶ Hail Mary…

The path of the righteous is like the light of dawn, which shines brighter and brighter until full day. PROVERBS 4:18

▶ Hail Mary…

Blessed is anyone who endures temptation. Such a one has stood the test and will receive the crown of life that the Lord has promised to those who love him. JAMES 1:12

▶ Hail Mary…

Whoever exalts himself will be humbled, and whoever humbles himself will be exalted. MATTHEW 23:12

▶ Hail Mary…

I have fought the good fight, I have finished the race, I have kept the faith. Henceforth there is laid up for me the crown of righteousness. 2 TIMOTHY 4:7-8

▶ Hail Mary…

I will cause your name to be celebrated in all generations; therefore the peoples will praise you for ever and ever. PSALM 45:17

▶ Hail Mary…

▶ Glory Be to the Father…

▶ O My Jesus…

▶ Hail, Holy Queen…

ABOUT THE ARTWORK

Flemish Renaissance artist Simon Bening (1483-1561) was one of the most famous "illuminators" of his time. Bening painted the small pictures or miniatures in illuminated manuscripts, books written by hand and decorated with fully colored paintings and elaborate borders. His work, which was in high demand by the most powerful ruling families of Europe, is characterized by figures with small hands and rounded heads, faces that portray emotion, clothing that accurately depicts texture, and landscapes with skilled perspectives.

The artwork in this book is taken from *The Stein Quadriptych*, a series of sixty-four miniatures on parchment pasted on four wooden panels. The miniatures represent scenes from the life of Christ and the Virgin Mary. It is unclear whether the miniatures were taken from a manuscript or were originally conceived as an altarpiece. In either case, they functioned as devotional aids, urging the viewer to meditate on the miracle of the Incarnation and the Passion and Resurrection of Christ. *The Stein Quadriptych* is part of the collection of The Walters Art Museum, Baltimore, Maryland.

Also available from The Word Among Us Press

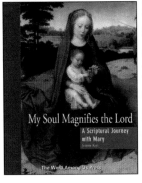

My Soul Magnifies the Lord:
A Scriptural Journey with Mary
Jeanne Kun

Follow Mary step by step in her pilgrimage of faith and deepen your own faith in the process! This unique book focuses on ten important gospel scenes in the life of the Blessed Virgin Mary, from her *fiat* at the Annunciation to her presence in the upper room at Pentecost. Each chapter includes: a poetic meditation; the Scripture passage to be studied; a series of questions for delving deeper into the meaning and significance of each scene; and questions for applying these truths to our own lives.

To order this and other fine books from
The Word Among Us Press, log on to
www.wordamongus.org,
call 1-800-775-9673,
or visit your local Catholic bookstore.